I0419954

....

....

....

....

....

Designed by Andreea Chiriac

www.ingramcontent.com/pod-product-compliance
Lightning Source LLC
Chambersburg PA
CBHW070425290526
45791CB00005B/1837
9781074006372